A World in Danger

HOTTER

By
Brenda McHale

PowerKiDS press™
New York

Published in 2022 by The Rosen Publishing Group, Inc.
29 East 21st Street, New York, NY 10010

This edition is published by arrangement with Booklife Publishing

Edited by:
Madeline Tyler

Designed by:
Gareth Liddington

Cataloging-in-Publication Data

Names: McHale, Brenda.
Title: Hotter / Brenda McHale.
Description: New York : PowerKids Press, 2022. | Series: A world in danger | Includes glossary and index.
Identifiers: ISBN 9781725336018 (pbk.) | ISBN 9781725336032 (library bound) | ISBN 9781725336025 (6 pack) | ISBN 9781725336049 (ebook)
Subjects: LCSH: Heat waves (Meteorology)--Juvenile literature. | Forest fires--Juvenile literature. | Climatic changes--Juvenile literature.
Classification: LCC QC981.8.A5 M343 2022 | DDC 551.5'253--dc23

Manufactured in the United States of America

CPSIA Compliance Information: Batch #CWPK22. For Further Information contact Rosen Publishing, New York, New York at 1-800-237-9932.

PHOTO CREDITS

Cover & Throughout – Vladyslav Trenikhin, Weerachai Khamfu, Christian Roberts-Olsen, SoleilC, Imageman, 2 – Lumppini, 4&5 – Patrick Foto, tandemich, 6&7 – narongpon chaibot, Dima Zel, 8&9 – RickDeacon, Ody_Stocker, 10&11 – muratart, AndreAnita, 12&13 – Warren Metcalf, JIANG TIANMU, 14&15 – Christian Roberts-Olsen, Leonid Andronov, 16&17 – Richard Whitcombe, Rich Carey, 18&19 – Wim Hoek, FloridaStock, 20&21 – Monkey Business Images, Vladimir Ya, 22&23 – Wang An Qi, Monkey Business Images, BlueBoeing, Pressmaster.

Images are courtesy of Shutterstock.com. With thanks to Getty Images, Thinkstock Photo and iStockphoto.

CONTENTS

Words that look like this can be found in the glossary on page 24.

ARE WEATHER AND CLIMATE DIFFERENT?

Weather is what happens day to day. We may talk about it raining or being sunny when we're talking about weather.

Climate is what the weather is like over a long time. We talk about a hot place or a cold place when we're talking about climate.

WHAT IS CLIMATE CHANGE?

The global climate is changing. In different places around the world it is getting hotter, wetter, windier, and drier.

Let's have a look at why it's getting hotter and what that means for Earth and the things that live here.

WHY IS EARTH GETTING HOTTER?

Carbon dioxide is a greenhouse gas.

Earth is getting hotter because of gases going into the air. We call these greenhouse gases.

Some of the gases come from burning fossil fuels to make electricity and to heat our homes. We also use fossil fuels to power many vehicles.

WHY ARE THEY CALLED GREENHOUSE GASES?

Greenhouse gases keep the heat from the sun from escaping the atmosphere. They make a bubble around Earth like a greenhouse, which keeps all the heat inside.

We can't open the windows on the greenhouse we've made around Earth!

This is called the greenhouse effect, and it's quickly making Earth warmer. This is a problem because many plants and animals can't adapt quickly enough to the changing temperature.

SNOW LEOPARD

The snow leopard is vulnerable. It lives in high mountains in Asia where it often snows. It's adapted to live in the snow some of the time.

If the snow leopard dies out, the rest of its food chain will change.

As Earth is getting warmer, snow is melting. The snow leopard's habitat is getting smaller and this makes it harder for them to survive.

Snow leopards eat wild goats and other smaller animals.

WILDFIRES

Fires start more easily and spread more quickly when it's hot and dry. They can burn across huge areas. People and animals can be killed, and habitats and homes can be destroyed.

CALIFORNIAN FOREST FIRES

In California, wildfires were worse in 2015 than they had ever been before. Over 15,400 square miles (40,000 sq km) of California's land were burned.

IS THE SEA GETTING HOTTER?

A healthy reef is full of life.

Coral is made of sea creatures that look a bit like rock. They grow together in big areas called reefs. Lots of sea creatures need coral reefs to feed on and hide in.

Coral is being harmed by warmer seas. Reefs are already dying off. If the reefs don't survive, many creatures will lose their food and habitats.

This reef has already died.

WHAT'S HAPPENING IN COLD PLACES?

Ice in colder areas is melting. This is causing huge ice sheets and glaciers to break up in places such as Antarctica. It is also making sea levels rise, which can cause flooding.

Polar bears might die out if there is no ice.

Polar bears eat seals that live on the ice. If there is less ice, it means there will be fewer seals for the polar bears to eat.

IS IT TOO LATE TO SLOW CLIMATE CHANGE?

Climate change is happening, but we can slow it down. People from around the world can work together!

Nobody wants to hurt Earth by making it hotter. Each of us can do something to make things better. One of the best things to do is to tell other people what you know. Let's spread the word!

HOW CAN WE HELP?

To slow climate change, we need to make fewer greenhouse gases. That means we need to find new ways to make electricity and power vehicles.

Here are two things you can do to help fight climate change:

Turn off the lights when you're not using a room.

Ask to walk or ride bikes for short trips.

GLOSSARY

adapt to change over time to suit the environment

atmosphere the mixture of gases that make up the air and surround Earth

food chain a series of living things that rely on each other for food

fossil fuels fuels, such as coal, oil, and gas, that formed millions of years ago from the remains of animals and plants

gases matter, like air, which fills any space available

glaciers extremely large amounts of ice that move slowly

global relating to the whole world

habitat the natural home in which animals, plants, and other living things live

vehicle things used to move people or things from one place to another

vulnerable likely to become endangered (in danger of dying out completely)

INDEX